Christie is unapologetically real, raw, and oh so relatable as she takes us on a journey through her past disappointments, present wins, and future goals. Reading this book, I could feel the emotions behind her experiences and understand her passion to see couples of all stages succeed. As she dives into real-life topics such as communication, finances, and faith, she brings the words "for better or worse" to life! This marriage book is truly life-changing and so exciting that it's hard to put down!

—Janrod and Joanie Bagalay

7 years married

Life of Faith

marriage UNCUT

Real Marriage Transformation and Preparation

CHRISTIE AMOYO

MARRIAGE UNCUT
Copyright © 2021 by Christie Amoyo

All rights reserved. Neither this publication nor any part of this publication may be reproduced or transmitted in any form or by any means, electronic or mechanical, including photocopying, recording or any information storage and retrieval system, without permission in writing from the author.

All Scripture quotations, unless otherwise indicated, are taken from the Holy Bible, New International Version®, NIV®. Copyright ©1973, 1978, 1984, 2011 by Biblica, Inc.™ Used by permission of Zondervan. All rights reserved worldwide. www.zondervan.com The "NIV" and "New International Version" are trademarks registered in the United States Patent and Trademark Office by Biblica, Inc.™ Scripture quotations marked (NLT) are taken from the Holy Bible, New Living Translation, copyright ©1996, 2004, 2007, 2013, 2015 by Tyndale House Foundation. Used by permission of Tyndale House Publishers, Inc., Carol Stream, Illinois 60188. All rights reserved. Scripture quotations marked (KJV) are taken from the Holy Bible, King James Version, which is in the public domain.

Softcover ISBN: 978-1-4866-2044-9
Hardcover ISBN: 978-1-4866-2045-6
eBook ISBN: 978-1-4866-2046-3

Word Alive Press
119 De Baets Street, Winnipeg, MB R2J 3R9
www.wordalivepress.ca

Cataloguing in Publication may be obtained through Library and Archives Canada

Contents

Foreword	ix
Introduction	xi

Part One

1.	Us	1
2.	Our Proposal and Wedding	7
3.	Year One, Month One	15
4.	Work, Family, and Everything Else	19
5.	With or Without Hope	27
6.	Our Choice, No One Else's	35

Part Two

7.	Session One, The Past	43
8.	Session Two, The Present	55
9.	Session Three, The Future	65
10.	Never Give Up	73

Advance praise for *Marriage Uncut*

Pastor Christie has written a very real book about marriage. She shares personal details about her life and marriage with incredible grace and honesty. Her wisdom and advice is absolute truth, and the couple who wants a successful marriage will take these words to heart.

For the engaged couple, this is a book you should read and take seriously. It's easy for an engaged couple to think they will never go through hard times like these, but I promise that you will. Follow the advice laid out in this book so that *when* the storms come, you are not caught off-guard.

For the couple who is already married, I'm sure you've already had some disappointments or gone through some things you thought you never would. Maybe you're in a good season, or maybe your marriage is barely hanging on; the principles laid out in this book are for everyone.

This book will help you identify where the cracks are in your marriage so you can fix them and be better prepared for the future. Wherever you're at, please read this book with an open mind and heart to receive everything God has for you from it.

—Bob and Andrea Ewonchuk
15 years married

Whether you're considering marriage, are newlyweds, or have been married for a long time, this book is for you! Pastor Christie's raw and honest stories about her own marriage provide you with the comfort of knowing that marriage will always be a work in progress. Her book includes great applications that have allowed us to sit down and analyze our own relationship. It's even given us many moments to laugh together and at each other, which is definitely something every marriage could use more of!

—Jermaine and Bernadene Bagalay
5 years married

My husband and I are in our second year of marriage and it… is… tough. Reading this book made us feel a little less disappointed in ourselves. We saw that our struggles, frustrations, and impossible expectations of each other are normal… and that the storms we face in our marriage will only make us stronger!

In this book, Christie openly shares their story to help minister to others. From those prepping for marriage, to those weathering current marriage storms, and to those who need healing from past marriage storms, she helps us to see that God uses all these bumps in the journey of marriage to create the beautiful road to your happily ever after!

—Harrizon and Eileen Andasan
2 years married

Just real—that's what this book is from start to finish. A real life story of two people who are choosing to actively put work and energy into their marriage and are seeing the rewards and God's faithfulness for doing so. The book is full of practical wisdom if you're just starting out, and full of encouraging reminders to keep going if you're further along in the journey.

—Scott and Mandy Stewart
12 years married

Foreword

First of all, I would like to let everyone know that I am the man I am today because of my wife. I'm a firm believer that every successful man has a powerful loving wife right by his side, and that is a key to a man's success in life and a family's success. Be it myself or our children, my wife is the main reason we are able to succeed in everything we face, as her faith in Christ is stubborn and unmovable.

If you have read Christie's previous books, you know that her faith in Christ is her foundation and motivation to believe God for the impossible and the miraculous. Well, it is this determination and her attitude of love and encouragement that has helped us as a married couple and family to survive the many obstacles she shares throughout this book.

God has done an amazing work in our lives. He has helped us overcome so many things that have tried to break up our marriage and our personal lives.

We believe that as we share these practical and true testimonies in our journey, you will come to know that we are normal people just like you. I believe when a couple first begins their married life, they truly do believe it will be happily ever after and that everything will be perfect. Although that might be the plan, sometimes life hits hard and unexpectedly, and we want to encourage you that there's something you can do to prepare and navigate through those times to see yourselves grow deeper in love with each other—and more importantly, with God.

My wife has been an amazing encouragement to me. I will be the first to admit that I haven't always been the best husband or father and that I have struggled with knowing what a godly man even is. But Christie has always been there to pray for me, love me, and help me face my fears and shortcomings.

We have learned as a couple that we are different, as I believe all couples are. That makes it difficult, because sometimes that's what causes the tension. But we now know that it's actually part of God's amazing plan. With our differences, we have the ability to solve difficulties if we learn to use each other's strengths to complement our weaknesses instead of trying to overpower each other.

I know this book will bring many scenarios to light in your life and I pray it will be an inspiration to you and let you know that marriage can be better. It can be the best part of your life as you walk your journey today!

—Danrey Amoyo

Introduction

Every time we meet up with a new couple for their upcoming wedding, we relive our own. If we're asked to counsel the couple and prepare them for marriage, it's really a self-examination of how our own marriage is going. The things we discuss with the couple eagerly anticipating their wedding day and their life together touch our own hearts. After a session is over and we're left alone, we reflect and open up again about the issues in our marriage that we too are facing, or the great victories we have come through.

When it's time for the couple's big day, I hear my husband joyfully talk about the union God has brought together and the blessings have been placed upon it. He then adds a few stories of our own and speaks of his gratefulness for our marriage.

I'm constantly overwhelmed with love, forgiveness, and gratitude for our life together, even when it hasn't been perfect. I don't think any marriage can ever be perfect, unless your definition is different than mine. I know life doesn't ever feel or look perfect, so why do we think our marriages could live up to those expectations?

What I'm grateful for is that we can look back and see that our foundation has been made stronger through all sorts of challenges over time. This causes us to look ahead and see great victory.

In this book, I don't intend to tell you the right things you should do to have a happy marriage and happy life. I believe that you choose what you want. Two separate lives are coming together and working at being one—and in disagreements, there is opportunity.

Marriage isn't easy and you need to put an overwhelming amount of effort into it. The rewards that come from a marriage that's lived on purpose will far exceed your expectations and give you a great vision for your future.

Part One

In this first half of this book, I want you to see who my husband Danrey and I were, and who we are becoming as a couple. No, we haven't arrived at perfection in ourselves or our marriage, but we're taking steps to better it every day.

We all start somewhere, and Danrey and I want to share with you the real-life dramas and victories we have gone through which have formed who we are as individuals and as a couple.

God has created us all to be unique and placed us where we can choose to grow in our faith, our family, and our finances—first apart, and then together. The purpose of marriage is to multiply and enhance the gifts and blessings God has so graciously given us.

chapter one

Us

My Story

I GREW UP WITH JUST MY MOTHER. SHE AND MY FATHER WEREN'T married, but she still had a good relationship with him, which allowed me to have a good relationship with him.

When I turned eight, my mother chose to marry my stepfather of now thirty years. She couldn't have married a more amazing man; he showed me what marriage means in such a beautiful way. He absolutely adored my mother. For these past thirty years of my life, he has never raised his voice at my mother, myself, or my children in any situation that has ever arisen in our household.

Growing up, I never thought much about marriage until the day I told God that the next person I dated was the one I would marry. I was nineteen years old and had already lived a life separate from biblical truths about marriage and the covenant that's made between a man and a woman. Unfortunately, I had been exposed to pornography and inappropriate situations when I was just a little girl. I carried that through my teenage years and had an extremely skewed picture of what a proper husband and wife relationship should look like.

When I was fifteen, I was invited by my best friend to go to a church youth group. At this time, only my grandmother was a Christian and she talked to me about God. She knew Him in such an honest and real way; He had saved her from the bondage of alcohol. Now she had made it her mission to listen to God and pray for people every moment of the day.

She attended this church I had been invited to, which made me even more inclined to go there with my friend.

After a few weeks of attending this Friday night youth group, I took the opportunity to pray with the pastor's wife. That prayer changed my life. I prayed for my mom, stepdad, and dad to all stop drinking, a curse that was rampant in our families. I thought this was an impossible prayer, thinking, *How could God ever answer this prayer?* But to my complete surprise, within one month all of my parents had stopped drinking. To this day, twenty-three years later, they have never turned back and they all have a personal relationship with Jesus!

When this prayer was answered, I knew in my heart that God must be real.

My family started to go to church, the same one I had being going to. Throughout the weeks, I made attempts to include God and church into my regular, very secular teenage life.

This all came to a crossroads one day, for you can't live two separate ways and pretend everything is okay. After a weekend of partying, I went to church with my parents, and that day I felt worse than ever. I didn't want to be there, I didn't want to talk to God, and I wanted to give up this whole Christianity thing.

That's when He spoke to me. While in the bathroom, I looked at myself in the mirror, feeling miserable, and heard Him speak loud and clear inside me: *You are becoming exactly what you hated.*

The life my parents led had put me on an emotional rollercoaster. I loved them so much and hated seeing them hurt from the decisions they were making. I'd always thought to myself that I would never become like them. I didn't want to be in that lifestyle of partying, alcohol, and destructive behaviour.

So those words I heard pierced me so deep. Truth can hurt enough to make you do something about it. I had to make a choice that day, and I walked away knowing my life would never be the same.

After that, I wanted to know everything there was to know about God. Since I was graduating high school, I enrolled myself in the first Bible college that came across my path. This college was located in a very small town outside Winnipeg, and I thought its seclusion would be perfect for me.

That was it. I was on a mission. I left my friends and family behind and moved to college, where I knew no one and knew nothing of what career I wanted to pursue. All I knew was that I could enroll in business classes, because I liked math, and make friends in my dorm and play on the volleyball team.

While at college, I had some relationships that still weren't right. They tried knocking on my door, metaphorically, to get my attention. Eventually I just didn't answer them anymore.

When God answered my prayer at fifteen, showed me love and care, and then chose to speak to me, I knew He needed all my attention. I told Him I didn't want to waste any more of myself or my time on dating.

I attended some special group sessions for those who wanted prayer for past sexual abuse or promiscuity, and it was nice to know I wasn't the only one who had made mistakes of this nature. But the greatest thing was getting confirmation of the Father's love for His daughters and understanding how He restores and heals these areas of our lives.

I enjoyed going to this college, getting to know God more, and reading the Bible. I made friends and enjoyed my social life on campus. I didn't plan on getting into any relationships there, even though it was often coined "bridal college" by others.

His Story (in a Nutshell)

My husband Danrey grew up in a home where his parents had been married from the beginning—not of time, but the start of his life. They faced many challenges in their early years. They'd both come to Canada from the Philippines, but at different times and from different religions. My husband was the eldest child, and when his sister came along her health was at the forefront of everyone's minds and hearts. He had a little brother, too. Overall, Danrey's life at home was quite hectic.

Their family saw many miracles take place over the years and through the storms, and these miracles brought them all to a true knowledge of Christ.

Danrey was involved in sports and the church music team, and he had a large and close family.

In the midst of his normal life, he was also exposed to pornography and inappropriate behaviour when he was young, and although he had a churched family he didn't know the value and importance of some of the decisions he had made. He got involved in the wrong crowd at school, and immediately his parents found him a Christian high school to attend. There, he made some great friends.

Apparently we had just missed each other at the same youth group and church. My family had left to join my aunt at another church. I guess it just wasn't our time to meet yet!

He soon found interest in youth ministries and found a Bible college that had a great basketball program. And as you may have guessed, he too picked the same secluded Christian college.

Our Story

We met in college during our freshman year, and in all honesty I assumed he liked my roommate, a Filipino girl. I thought that was why he hung around us often. Later on, I found out the truth. I probably should have guessed it by him coming to every one of my volleyball games to cheer me on.

We were both very independent and had our lives planned out, but we found our independence in different ways. I grew up not having to share my room, my things, or my parents. His independence meant leaving home and finally having his own things and making his own decisions.

Danrey was the one friend of mine who actually had a car in college. That was a big deal. He was happy to offer to drive me back to Winnipeg when he went home to visit.

Being good friends with someone, and not thinking about the possibility of dating, really allows you to open up to someone and get to know them better. It also allows you to be completely yourself and totally silly. He was the silly one!

When we decided to start a relationship, he was aware of the commitment I had made to God, so if he wanted to now date me it meant he was going to marry me too.

We dated for a year—and then got married.

chapter two

Our Proposal and Wedding

GETTING MARRIED WASN'T AS SIMPLE AS IT SOUNDED. I'M someone who writes lists and checks things off, so that was probably the easy part. It was the things we didn't have control over that caused problems.

I had pictured him proposing to me over and over again. I waited for the whole summer, thinking and imagining this event. But it didn't happen. I'd thought it would for sure happen on my birthday, and around that time his grandmother became very ill. I really saw his sensitive side come out. He asked me to pray with him for his grandma (lola), a cute little woman who never spoke any English to me; I learned how to say a few words in Tagalog.

One day, his grandmother was talking to Danrey when I wasn't around and mentioned something to him about his Filipino girlfriend. He laughed so hard at this. You see, she had always worn her sunglasses, both in and out of the house, so she'd thought I was a bit darker-skinned than I was. We all laughed together about this.

When she got sick and ended up in the hospital, Danrey and I bought her two little stuffed bears, one brown and one tan, to resemble us by her bedside. She ended up passing away that summer, and her funeral took place on my birthday.

My cousin was getting married that October, and she asked me to watch her apartment while they went away on their honeymoon. It was Thanksgiving and we had all sorts of family functions and dinners planned that same weekend. I also got the flu.

Apparently, during this time of family functions, Danrey snuck away and showed my family the ring he'd bought and asked my dad for permission to marry me. I cannot imagine the look on my dad's face, but he said yes and gave Danrey a big hug!

The following day, in the rain, he picked me up to take me to his house for Thanksgiving. He pulled the car over and we walked up a new pretty bridge that had just been built in Winnipeg. As we reached the middle of it, we closed our eyes and he prayed with me.

"God, help me to do what I'm about to do," he said.

When I opened my eyes, he was on his knee with a beautiful ring in his hand.

I said yes and then we ran back to the car because it was raining and I felt sick. He then took me to a local restaurant and we had breakfast together and talked wedding plans.

Let the Planning Begin

We loved each other and loved the idea of being together for the rest of our lives. I had already made the commitment to be a part of his church, where he was a drummer in the band. He was going to college to be a youth pastor and this was where he would work afterwards.

Our Proposal and Wedding

It was a big deal for us to go, since I was one of only two Caucasians there. They also spoke mostly in Tagalog and I didn't understand one bit of it.

But God is so good. I got involved in the youth group there with Danrey and loved it. I loved being with the girls. God had put such a sensitive spot in my heart for all those young girls who were really struggling in their family and home situations. I felt like I had found a huge part of my calling in the church body.

So we had the church question checked off.

Next, we didn't really know when the wedding would be. He wasn't set to graduate for another two years, and that was just too long to wait. We decided that once the school year was over, we could get married. My job at the time would sustain us if we got an apartment close by, and Danrey could work weekends and get a job for the summertime.

We had a plan.

It was fun looking at apartments in the area, and then we finally signed a lease. After all the renovations the owners wanted to do, they told us we could get in by May 1. Well, that sounded like a great month to get married, and it was right after the end of his school year.

So May 3 ended up being the wedding date.

* * *

As we were planning for the wedding, someone dear to me passed away. My grandma—well, my step-grandma—had been sick for a long time and didn't tell any of her family.

I was very close with her, and she had always been well aware of the love in the air between me and Danrey. She'd asked who this man was in my life and I showed her pictures of him and told her all our plans. She'd kept telling me, and everyone else, just how handsome he was and that she couldn't wait to have dinner with us soon.

She never got to meet him. It was an extremely sad time for me.

My family didn't know what to do with all of her belongings and asked if we wanted to take her table and a few other things. I was honoured they had thought of us and as a result my grandma left me with some really nice things. She would have wanted to give us everything anyway. She was wonderful.

* * *

Although I had checked out a few wedding magazines, I focused on the main bookings. We looked for a venue down the street from the church, and ended up finding the perfect place with an old ballroom and gigantic chandeliers. We also decided to have a lunch reception instead of the whole dancing and party evening. We wanted this to be really simple and straight to the point for us and our guests. We also didn't want everyone to wait around all day after the ceremony to share a meal with us and celebrate. No one we knew had done a lunch reception.

We were blessed with all the other details, to the point that I'd say the planning really wasn't stressful. I was too excited to stress about it. We were going to enjoy every minute of our wedding.

The next thing I did was shop for my gown. I had a style in mind, and after going to just two stores, which were located side by side, I came out of the dressing room wearing a simple, fitted, sparkly gown. The look on my mom's face told me this was the one. The shop owner asked for a deposit, but my mother had saved the tiny bits of rent I'd been paying her as I lived at home after college and used it to pay for my dress on the spot.

Thank you, Mom, and thank you, Jesus!

The day we headed out to the florist, my grandmother called and told me she would pay for all my flowers. Wow, another blessing! I had decided that my bouquet of tulips had to have two red roses in it, to remind us of both of our grandmothers who wouldn't get to be there on our special day.

I worked at a pottery supplies and gift store at the time, and I found my little giveaways there and all the pretty wedding stationary we needed. I also got the opportunity to use my boss's beautiful old Impala for our wedding car. He decorated it with fancy signs and bows.

> MOST PEOPLE'S PLANNING SEEMS TO GO INTO THE ACTUAL DAY AND NOT THE ACTUAL MARRIAGE.

The wonderful thing about this was the fact that my dad was a car guy and he gladly offered to drive us around on our wedding day!

My in-laws-to-be arranged for the videographer, my friends served as the photographers, and our friends and family sang some songs. The girls' dresses were being made, the food was all picked, and the spending wasn't out of control.

Danrey already had worked out his details, like the rings, his tux, and the sound system. It was going to be great.

We had gone through all of our pre-marriage counselling and planned for life to be hunky dory together. After all, most people's planning seems to go into the actual day and not the actual marriage.

Our Day

Well, let's start with the night before. My maid of honour burnt a hole in her dress with the iron, but thank God we took the little shawl she had and made a fabric pouf that resembled a flower or bow and attached it to the area with the hole. Voi-la... a snazzy new look for her dress!

The girls slept at my house the night before, and my wonderful hairdresser friend came over at 6:00 a.m. There seemed to be a lot of people in and out of the house for a few hours, and then the decorated Impala pulled up. I had butterflies in my tummy!

As my dad drove me through downtown, I saw a little girl in the back seat of another car staring at me and smiling. When I waved at her, I felt like the queen.

We got to the church and hid downstairs until it was time. In the stairway, my dad looked at me and told me I was beautiful; it was something I had always craved to hear him say.

That's when everything hit me and tears filled my eyes. Moments like that seemed to stop time in its tracks.

I chose to honour both my dad and my stepdad and have them walk me down the aisle together and give me away, since they'd both played such important roles in my life. I didn't realize the impact this had on my mother at the time.

Then there he was: my husband-to-be, staring at me as I walked down the aisle.

There are definitely some aesthetic choices and program issues I wish I would have changed, looking back, but they didn't really matter.

Our Proposal and Wedding

As we exited after the ceremony, we were attacked with rice. I'd bought bubbles, but whatever. We then got into the car to do a little victory lap around the downtown area.

When we got back, my family had left for the reception so I didn't get to have photos with them. I think they must have just been excited. Danrey's family, on the other hand, loves taking lots and lots of photos and were waiting for our return.

Our reception was great. My husband surprised me and sang me a song. To this day, it's the only time he's ever sung to me.

After many hugs and speeches, it was all over. Even with the venue forgetting to put our parents at the head table with us, everything went smoothly and we got $1,000 off our bill for their mistake. Bonus!

Our free room at the hotel was small and perfect. Because we'd had a lunch reception, we then had the whole evening to ourselves to reminisce about our big day.

Now it felt like we could relax and enjoy the rest of our lives. Spending the night together, ordering our first meal together (Chinese food), and signing my new name confirmed that we had entered a whole new season.

Everything was exciting and new—so new that it even felt a little fake, a little embarrassing. Shocking, in many ways.

The honeymoon stage is full of a lot of love and a lot of firsts. This includes trying to figure out and accept all the differences between you and come to terms with everything that isn't necessarily going your way anymore. When you're married you have to take someone else into consideration, their likes and dislikes, their thoughts and emotions.

After our honeymoon, every day to follow wasn't necessarily the best day ever. In fact, some didn't even seem to be that good. We were learning.

chapter three

Year One, Month One

The day after we were married, we took all our belongings out of the hotel room and brought them to our apartment. It had been waiting for us for a few weeks while it underwent some small renovations.

To our surprise, we walked inside to find our black furniture covered in white from the renovations that still hadn't been completed. No worries; we would talk to the landlord and give him another few days while we went away on our honeymoon.

For our honeymoon, we headed to a little couples resort just outside the city. It was a comfortable and enjoyable place to spend a few quiet days before we jumped back into our regular schedules.

But before we could check in at the resort, we had some time to kill. Danrey took me along on a trip to buy himself a home entertainment system—I mean buy it for *us*. We needed a nice home entertainment system and we put it on financing. That was something new for me. My parents hadn't used credit, so I was used to paying for things with cash. Even my education had been all paid for by the time we got married. This was something we would need to address in our marriage.

But not during the honeymoon stage.

When we got home from our honeymoon, we were able to settle into our nice little apartment and make it home. The very first morning, I awoke to find that Danrey wasn't beside me. I heard noise from the TV, and there he was playing video games in the living room.

I had no idea he even liked video games, I thought to myself. *Is this what I have to look forward to?*

I thought grown-ups didn't play video games, especially newly married ones. That season for him thankfully didn't last too long. But the games were really nice to have. When his siblings and their friends slept over at our apartment, it gave them something to do.

For the first two weeks, we didn't do much cooking and ate out all the time. We went out with our friends and stayed up late.

But soon it was time to settle down and get to work. It was really interesting to sample each others' food choices and cooking inventions. I tried his sardines and he tried my hot dog wraps. We had a lot to learn. It was easier to go to our parents' places for dinner and take some leftovers home. We did miss their cooking!

Because he was still a student and had another year of classes to finish, he got a great summer job working at a hospital. It wasn't the nicest job, but it had great hours and great pay. He woke up early every morning and often rode his bike to work, and he got home early in the day. It was a great routine.

We were both involved in church, with him leading the youth group and playing drums as part of the worship team.

Exactly one month after we were married, while heading to worship practice with two of the youth, a drunk driver came across his path and they had a very severe crash. Danrey broke his wrist. The boy in the front passenger seat had no major injuries, but the airbag hit him and he was sore and shaken up. The boy in the middle of the back seat had felt pressure as he flew forward and hit the dashboard with his head, cutting his forehead open. The car was totalled, but they were all going to be okay. Thank you, Jesus.

Danrey couldn't work after the accident, so he went on employment insurance and we learnt very quickly how to balance our budget. We had to start by creating one! We had just assumed we were living within our means and could therefore spend what we wanted and trust everything to work out on its own. But if you don't put effort into your finances, they won't balance. Anything you don't put effort into maintaining will automatically deteriorate; this can be said for every area of your life and walk with Christ.

> ANYTHING YOU DON'T PUT EFFORT INTO MAINTAINING WILL AUTOMATICALLY DETERIORATE.

Danrey ended up losing his position at the hospital and had to look for a different avenue of making money. He soon found out that he was a really good car salesman and he excelled during the short time he worked at a local dealership.

The pressure was on. After all, my job was only part-time and there was no opportunity for promotion there. I worked at a family gift store, which made me very happy, but I had always tried taking on other jobs on the side to make more money.

Not long after Danrey started up at school again, we were told he would have to take an additional course in order to earn the youth group position he had been promised from the beginning. Okay. But the student loans were starting to pile up. He'd assumed he would get a lot of help to pay off his loans once his education was finished and that the new job would pay well enough.

We may have gotten married young, but it sure felt like we had to grow up fast. The decisions we had to make, the situations we faced, and even the energy we had were all drained in our first month. We hadn't been ready to make all these decisions well, but as we made them we became a great team and were able to enjoy each other and have fun together during our honeymoon stage.

chapter four

Work, Family, and Everything Else

DANREY FINALLY FINISHED HIS EDUCATION. HE TRANSFERRED TO a college in Winnipeg and didn't take full course loads, which enabled him to play basketball for the college an extra year. But that made my husband happy and it gave us some entertainment during the season.

We were still the young, fun married couple in college together and the church soon hired him to be the youth pastor. But the position didn't provide for us like we'd thought it would. We would make it work, though.

For the next five years, my husband made that job his number one priority. It was an exciting and yet frustrating time in our marriage. I loved being a part of the church, being involved with everything my husband was involved with. He spent all his time with the youth, the worship team, or janitorial duties. If someone told him to jump, he asked, "How high?"

He figured that all his hard work was pleasing to God—and if not, at least everyone else around him was pleased.

Except me.

For years, I went to family functions by myself because my husband had to be at church. I could see a big rift between the church's expectations of him, the culture's expectation of him, and my expectations of him as a husband. After all, he and I were a team.

Our apartment was to undergo more renovations after our first year and we were given the opportunity to rent a friend's house. It was a tiny house, perfect for two—and now for our puppy. We didn't have children right away, but that dog was definitely practice; we gave her so much love and had to plan everything with her in mind.

We loved that little house and made it a home. But after a year went by, we had to move somewhere new. Without a place to go, we moved in with my parents. My husband didn't mind, but we felt like we were grasping at straws.

We'd thought we could maybe afford to buy our first house, but our bank quickly turned us down; we didn't make enough money.

One day, though, my husband saw a house listed for only $49,000. He was scared to tell me about it because it was far from my parents but closer to the church. It was actually pretty cute, and even smaller than the one we had just moved out of. But it looked nice.

Thankfully, the price was low enough for the bank to let us purchase it. We borrowed the down-payment from Danrey's parents and moved into our tiny blessed home.

Just having a place we could call our own felt great, and very few things needed upgrades or fixing. It became the youth hangout spot, and at times we'd have thirty young people in our tiny house at the same time. We all loved it.

We were really learning new things in our marriage at this time: owning our home, taking care of it, taking care of our dog, and maintaining two vehicles because of my long commute. We were figuring out how to live and work alongside each other. We had fun together and tried to enjoy every minute.

We did a lot of things side by side. Looking back, I see that a lot of it was on the surface. We didn't know how to work on our marriage, take care of it, or dream in it. We were living one day at a time, trying to make the most of every day. Any energy we had was put toward planning the youth ministry, and praying for and worrying about every youth in our care. The parents were very involved in our lives when things weren't going right with their children. Together, we navigated everything as best we knew how.

> WE DIDN'T KNOW HOW TO WORK ON OUR MARRIAGE, TAKE CARE OF IT, OR DREAM IN IT.

Over and over again, our parents and everyone else around us questioned when the first baby was going to come into the picture. But we weren't ready to start a family. We didn't desire to even be involved in the lives of others who had them. We just weren't baby people.

Until one day that all changed. One day, something sparked in us to talk about babies.

We were twenty-four and thought maybe this was the next thing to look forward to in our married lives. It would be a new thing, a new adventure, a new endeavour, a new challenge for us. We felt like life was going really well, and our busy and happy lives showed that we could handle something more.

The day soon came when we guessed that we were expecting. We were excited to go to the doctor to confirm our pregnancy.

I didn't feel too nauseous or tired yet, just a bit dizzy, but the doctor tested me and told me it was faintly positive.

Wow! We were excited, and over the next few days we leaked the surprise to our parents and family.

Not too long after, though, I started to have complications. Without going into all the details,[1] I underwent several tests, an extreme amount of pain and confusion, and an operation that ended the pregnancy.

Going through this sort of physical and emotional pain really does take you to a different level in your marriage. We were scared, unsure, happy, and then sad. I entered a period of depression during the weeks and months following the surgery. I didn't talk to my husband about too many things. In fact, I didn't want to talk about any of it. I pondered so many things in my head and in my heart.

Meanwhile, he was encouraging and happy and I didn't want to act like anything was wrong. I was tough and hid behind a smile.

My dog was the only consistent one. She remained normal and continued to be a little crazy. That's all I wanted: for things to just go back to normal. I wanted people to show their care but not treat me differently

Danrey definitely didn't know what to do in these silent times. He wanted to make me happy, so he just stood by my side and was helpful in every way.

We couldn't figure out how to navigate this period of time, so we just kept moving forward. We went on a holiday and stayed at a cabin by ourselves for a few days to focus on us again. We cleared our minds and were able to talk about our feelings a bit. It was very healing.

---

[1] You can find all the details in my first book, *The Promised Child*.

At the next doctor's visit, she explained that I shouldn't worry because we could try again in three months. What I'd gone through was a one in a million chance and it wouldn't happen again.

So in three months, I was pregnant again.

This time was completely different. I started off sick, nauseous, and tired. We had new hope, though, which took away a lot of the pain from the first loss.

As we started to plan for our future, we realized that our finances weren't in great shape. Even though we had a home and were making minimal payments, we were never on the same page when it came to saving and financial planning. I paid all the bills and Danrey wasn't too involved; he just expected things to get better. We were barely making ends meet.

We decided that because our house was small, in good shape, and we were having a baby, it was a perfect time to sell. We'd heard that the housing market was favourable to sellers and decided to put the house up for sale. It actually sold for $30,000 more than what we had purchased it for! Well, that was wonderful, but we hadn't found another home just yet so we moved in with my parents again.

We were happy to get rid of some debt and save some money during this time. We hadn't planned on staying with them after the baby was born, but I'm so happy we did. Sometimes things just don't go the way you plan, and having a baby is *huge*. Being with my parents was an amazing experience for us as husband and wife. It brought our marriage and planning to a whole new level.

Communication is so important at every stage in your marriage. Communication about the daily things will keep you in the loop of what's going on in each other's lives and help in terms of working through your thoughts and emotions.

We were bottled-up people. When I told him something was bothering me, it was when I had hit the limit. Then everything would come out at once. I'd been making a list of things in my head. He, on the other hand, kept everything to himself and didn't let me into his world, so I always felt separate from him. At the church with his friends, he had a life apart from us. He could separate me and our family from that other life, but I didn't have a life apart from him.

He and a few of the guys opened up a car shop and during this time he was very involved in that scene. I didn't like it. It seemed like he would spend a lot of time with it and would bring home car magazines. I cut out all the inappropriate pictures from them. He thought I was being a little overbearing, but by not allowing that kind of material in our home, in our eyes and in our hearts, I was trying to save myself from a lot of insecure thoughts and feelings.

You may think some things are little and insignificant, but they can actually turn into big deals in your marriage. They are deal-breakers, and they blind your eyes and harden your heart. I know that my husband worked for God a lot, but until God could break into his heart he was just stuck in the same patterns many religious people are stuck in.

God had given Danrey to me and I was determined to see God in every area of our lives. But God was going to have to show this to him, because I didn't want to be the nag and annoy him constantly.

If you think certain things are important to talk about in your marriage, they are. Don't ignore them or your heart and head won't be clear. If you need to forgive your spouse, forgive them.

Romans 12:18 says, *"If it is possible, as far as it depends on you, live at peace with everyone."* That peace is for you, too.

I wish I would have known these things then. I wish Danrey would have, too, but then I guess I wouldn't have anything to write about.

chapter five

With or Without Hope

It was wonderful when we got to be together as a family, but trying to navigate the world of church and its responsibilities was tedious. Danrey wasn't around a lot, and when he was it was only for moments at a time.

I thank God that Daniel, our first child, was a very easy baby. He just wanted Mom and was quiet and unfussy so we could take him many places with us. We had the opportunity to take him on a trip to Toronto with the leaders of our church. They all attended a conference while Daniel and I hung out at the hotel. It felt really nice being able to go away together, and Danrey and I tried to do our own thing on the day he had off.

While in Toronto, we got to meet up with my brother and spend a day with him and his daughter! What a blessing that was.

After this trip, my husband was supposed to plan a youth outreach trip to the Philippines. This hadn't been his idea and therefore he was a bit uncertain about it. He went because he was the youth pastor, but he didn't want to go and leave us behind. The Philippines is a long way from Canada, especially when you have a wife and a little boy waiting for you back home.

My parents happened to also be planning a trip to British Columbia, so I joined them there, which helped the time to pass more quickly.

During this trip was the first time I ever heard Danrey's voice crack. When we talked on the phone, he was choked up but didn't want to tell me how much he missed me.

We lived this way for the next few years. The trips he had to take, and the meetings that happened to fall on holidays, were always made a priority. We didn't put our own family needs ahead of the ministry—and when you can't help yourself, or fill yourself first, you'll never be able to help others.

> AND WHEN YOU CAN'T HELP YOURSELF, OR FILL YOURSELF FIRST, YOU'LL NEVER BE ABLE TO HELP OTHERS.

When our little guy was about one years old, we started house-hunting again. We wanted to be around the same area as the church so we could save time on Danrey's commute. We didn't have too much money set aside, but the house we wanted ended up being ours for only $87,000. We were moving up! We enjoyed the little three-bedroom home, but this was the point when we realized we had to get better at budgeting.

I still had my stable part-time job, and I created and sold pottery, paintings, and cosmetics on the side. I managed the house and our life with Daniel while Danrey was busy working. I was used to the routine and I even started to enjoy my time without him at home.

We were doing the best we could with what we had, but there was never any leftover money at the end of the day. It got to be pretty discouraging. I also had to sleep in my son's room so he would sleep through the night when the co-sleeping didn't work out.

We still had fun as a married couple and did life together, but we didn't spend enough time alone together or do anything to benefit our marriage. When we prayed together, it was usually at church or at the dinner table—or, the couch, as we watched TV and ate dinner.

I'm not trying to sound depressed, but we weren't planting many good seeds to help us build a great marriage. We just expected things to get better.

But they actually got worse.

Because our schedules were somewhat opposite and he did a lot of things without needing me around, I focussed on Daniel first. So Danrey and I started to grow apart.

I ended up getting pregnant again during this time, and we were hopeful about it. We knew having another child would add something great to our marriage and family.

But then we lost the baby and I became much more frustrated and introverted. The baby's heart had stopped beating and I had to go to the hospital. Combined with some other complications, I spent that whole month going back and forth between home and the hospital.

Danrey didn't know what to do or say, so he didn't do or say anything. I spent many days just wanting to sleep and not connect with him. I was trying hard to hold everything together on the outside, but every area of our lives seemed to suck. We were trapped and had no hope.

A few months later, we decided to try again and we ended up spending Christmas Eve of that year in the emergency room with another failed pregnancy. I was at the lowest I thought I could go.

Well, we were done. Danrey described it as feeling like he had a hole in him and it hurt. We didn't know what to think. He had to go to work like normally through this time, but I took as much time off as I needed. This was a very dark period in my life—and in our marriage and family.

What I didn't realize is that Danrey was starting to go down some roads that didn't do him any good. He started gaining a lot of weight and not caring for himself. He was so overwhelmed when the reality of our finances finally hit him that he didn't know what to do; he just felt the weight of the world on his shoulders and decided that he needed to fix it somehow. He didn't know how to help his wife.

We were so lost, so far away from God's truth and the reality of His love for us. We never prayed about our situations unless it was a desperate cry for help.

I wrote in my journal a lot at this time, sharing things with God but not my husband. I didn't want him to tell me to just get over everything and give me a hug when I didn't even feel close to him anymore.

I had started to notice how tired I was when I put Daniel to bed at night. I was so tired that I would want to sleep as well, but Danrey stopped coming to bed with me. He'd stay up late and watch TV. I would question him sometimes, because I knew this wasn't a good habit.

This was another example of how we were doing separate things when I felt like I needed him the most. I didn't realize that he had stopped caring about guarding his heart and mind at this point. He'd headed into his own form of depression.

He wasn't being truthful with me or faithful with some of the things he was choosing to watch. He opened the door to sin a little bit at a time, something which would eventually cause him to crash. He became a different person than the man I had married.

As we headed into our seventh year of marriage, I remember praying and thanking God. This was going to be our "year of perfection." I believed God was going to bless our marriage in so many ways. God's ways are not our own.

By this time, the arguing had started. I was happier when I wasn't around him, since we didn't seem to connect on any level. We were definitely just putting smiles on our faces when we went out.

He never liked it when I challenged him about things, so instead I tried to manipulate him with my attitude and actions. I wanted him to care about me and show it. I wanted him to feel bad when he let anger get the best of him. I was afraid when he raised his voice at me; that was one thing from my childhood that caused me to get scared.

One evening, everything seemed to blow up at home. Not only did he raise his voice, but he raised his hand. He didn't actually do anything, and I'm not even sure what I said, but I managed to go into the bathroom and close the door. I took a deep breath and contemplated taking my son and leaving him that night. It was one thing to raise his voice at me, but not while our son was near us. I wouldn't stand for that.

I prayed and told God that something needed to change right now or I would leave. I knew that would kick off a whole bunch of decisions I'd never before even contemplated making in my marriage—the marriage I had imagined since I was a girl.

I took a deep breath, gathered my thoughts, and opened the bathroom door. What I saw surprised me. There he was, sitting down, crying. God had gotten a hold of his heart at that moment and he apologized profusely, hugging me and not letting go.

My heart pounded as I hugged him back. I still wasn't sure.

Our son called from the other room where he was proud to show us the mess he had made with baby powder everywhere. My husband cradled us both and kept telling us over and over again how much he loved us. This was to be the start of something even deeper.

My grandmother often heard from God and let us know what He said. These messages were usually encouraging. This time when we spoke to her, she gave us a warning: she told Danrey that he had to tell me everything and not keep any secrets. She became very involved in speaking with him and encouraging me during this time.

Danrey still kept a lot of things inside him, but we tried to make things better, especially for the sake of our son.

One day, a visiting preacher came to our church. We hadn't known he was coming; it just so happened that our pastor had found out about him being in Winnipeg and invited him on a whim.

Well, this man came in with such a powerful presence that everyone he prayed for fell to the ground under the power of God. He had specific and personal words for people he didn't even know—and they were right on.

After the service, we were told to take him out for lunch, since the pastor and leadership were busy. This man definitely had something we didn't have, and I was nervous and excited to be able to spend more time with him.

When we got to the restaurant, the questions began. Is Daniel your only child? Are you going to have more? As I gently talked about our situation and told him we weren't going to have more children, his face began to change. He looked straight into my eyes and told me his faith testimony of his own grandchildren, twins who had been born despite the doctors saying they both wouldn't make it.

"You know why I'm telling you this, right?" he said.

> SATAN WAS GOING TO TRY EVERYTHING HE COULD TRY TO STOP THIS WORD FROM GETTING TO US, BECAUSE HE KNEW IT WOULD CHANGE OUR MARRIAGE AND FUTURE.

Hope welled up inside me and I just started to weep. The cry of my heart came out and I knew that God was up to something.

"You will have more children," the pastor said. That word stirred in my heart throughout the coming months and years.

We went home that day and talked about what kind of Christian this man was, how he'd had the boldness and courage to speak these words to us. And we questioned what it all meant.

Looking back now, I see that this is when the war began. Satan was going to try everything he could try to stop this word from getting to us, because he knew it would change our marriage and future.

Shortly after this visit, I got pregnant.

chapter six

Our Choice, No One Else's

I KEPT IN MY HEART THE WORD SPOKEN TO ME BY THAT PASTOR. It played over and over in my head and I knew something would be different this time around. We told God that we believed this word had come from Him and we were going to have our baby.

Danrey and I were invited to Hawaii to officiate for our friends' wedding. We said yes right away and started to plan the wedding with them. This was the first time we discussed our finances together, and we knew we would have to visit the doctor and have an ultrasound to make sure everything was going to be okay.

The ultrasound technicians said the two things I needed to hear: the baby had a strong heartbeat and was in the right spot! So the next thing we did was max out our credit card to pay for our Hawaii trip. My parents came with us, too. We had never been overseas and this was going to be a new experience.

During the trip, Danrey sat with me and apologized that for seven years he had never taken me on a trip. That was going to change. This became important to him. He knew his family needed him.

We had a wonderful trip, besides the nausea from the pregnancy. So much hope was starting to build inside me. I had many conversations with God, much contemplation and thinking. After all, I was pregnant and the doctors had told me not to get pregnant again.

The Christians around us told me to keep quiet about the pregnancy until we knew for sure things were going to be okay. To me, things had been okay as soon as those words had come out of the preacher's mouth!

When we got home from Hawaii, everything changed again.

In the weeks to follow, my husband entered a deep depression. He couldn't deal with everything that was going on in his mind and started to have panic attacks. The anxiety got so bad that he was sent to the hospital a number of times. The tests proved nothing was wrong, but his heart would start to beat so fast that his chest hurt.

He tried going to work at the church, and for a few days he'd be okay. Then another episode would hit. He didn't want to go out or speak too much, but his body just didn't feel right. He was convinced that he had some sort of stomach ulcer which was causing an incredible amount of heartburn. He needed pills for that. Then he was concerned that he wasn't sleeping properly, so he took pills for that, too.

And then one morning he woke up with Bell's palsy, nerve damage on one side of his face. His eye and lips drooped and he had pain in his ear which caused him so much discomfort. He was in and out of the hospital for two weeks before the symptoms subsided. To be free of it within two weeks was a miracle in itself.

At this point, we decided that we should sell our home again and pay off some debts while the housing market was still doing well. This was pretty humbling. It wasn't a big home, but it was still our home.

We had to move into my parents' home again so we could plan our next season.

This period of living with my parents brought us to the breaking point—not because living with them was rough (they provided wonderful support) but because Danrey's depression got so bad that he couldn't get out of bed. He took a lot of time off work and could barely eat for weeks; a meal would be one piece of toast with jam on it. Daniel and I became non-existent to him.

Danrey went on antidepressants and there was nothing I could do for him any longer. I prayed so much and trusted that God was going to do something. I kept hope, though, and thanked God for the baby growing inside me. His promise was alive and active in us.

When my in-laws and family came over to visit, they had their own family meetings with Danrey. I was not included, which added to my frustration.

I started to speak faith when everyone was speaking fear.

Finally the day came when my mom-in-law came over and got rid of my husband's pills. He didn't know what to do. He reacted in a fearful way at first, but then he started to hand it all over to God. He started to interact more with us and change up his destructive and hopeless behaviours.

Shortly after this time, he began to read the book *Battlefield of the Mind* by Joyce Meyer. As he opened himself to what God had to say to him through this book, and through all our prayers and encouragement, he began to change. Once he started to vocalize his feelings and let his thoughts and emotions out in a safe environment, things started to get better. His eyes opened to what he was doing to himself. It all started in the mind; your mind is the turning point that can make your heart and your whole life sick.

God led him into a new season where everything hiding in the closets came out. Much healing took place in his mind and heart. It was horrible and beautiful at the same time.

It took many months for him to recover physically, but mentally he had hope again. We had many, *many* talks about life and our future and priorities. We knew God had done something huge in our life. We listened to many encouraging testimonies and messages and started to get a real revelation of how good God is. We realized we had lost sight of who He was in our life. He was always with us; we had just stopped looking for Him.

When we had our baby and held him in our hands, we knew we had the proof. Faith in God's Word had brought him here to us. We were convinced we had been missing something in our Christian lives, and it all started to come together. After all, the Bible says that if we seek Him we shall find Him (Jeremiah 29:13). That's exactly what happened.

This is when we were introduced to a teaching from Pastor Gary Keesee that helped us with our new and simple faith life. It helped us to walk out our faith.

My mother had seen Pastor Keesee on a TV program and ordered his CD teaching series *Financial Revolution*. She passed the set on to us, hoping it would encourage us.

Well, it didn't just encourage us; it taught us how to renew our minds with the word of God and believe it first before believing any other way. This teaching was a breath of fresh air. And it wasn't just about finances. He also spoke of healing and experiencing breakthroughs in every area of life.

We started to apply what we'd learned to every area of our lives. Miracles weren't just for certain people at certain times anymore. Miracles are a way of life, intended for every child of God. That included us.

As husband and wife, we began to take on the world together. Not only did our health, finances, relationships, and church life change, but we came to agree on big and small decisions and catch a real vision for our lives. We realized that our words have so much power over us.

God answers prayers all the time, not sometimes. He is always speaking to us; it's just a matter of taking the time to listen. And if you can listen together and then do everything you can to keep your marriage the top priority, your family and everything else will benefit from the blessing of God upon it.

Our mindset changed as we chased after God, which brought us closer and closer together.

From what we learned along the way, and we're still recognizing and working through it, we have seen patterns in our life and marriage that continue to affect us. We need to be proactive about addressing these patterns.

> GOD ANSWERS PRAYERS ALL THE TIME, NOT SOMETIMES.

If I were to say that all our marriage problems were resolved at this point in our lives, that would be false. But we now had a great plan in place, a hope for our future together, so we could work through our difficulties as long as we were both willing.

Part Two

That was our story. Now what about yours?

In recent years, we started a new church. The vision for it came from a vision my grandmother had years before, of God repositioning us, and then the passion we developed in sharing with others the great things God was doing in our lives. You can trust Him to do it in yours, too! We figured that all the details would fall into place, and for the past eight years, they have been. And continue to do so.

One of the prayers we had was that God would show us how to build a pre-marriage plan for all those eagerly desiring to get married and have us officiate their wedding. And to those of you who are married already, I write this to encourage you: no matter what stage you're at in your marriage, you can reflect and respond to God and see things change and grow.

God literally dropped the outline for this plan into my head one day during prayer. As I wrote it all down, I saw how simple and powerful this was going to be.

Along with encouraging you to read books on marriage and never stop working at your marriage, we have a very simple and meaningful outline for you. There are so many moving parts in life, but this is a really simple plan you can use as an outline, filling in the blanks yourself as you move through life.

chapter seven

Session One, The Past

THERE ARE THREE THINGS YOU'LL CONSTANTLY HAVE TO ADJUST IN your own personal circumstances and unique situations in life:

1. Your family, friends, and relationships.
2. Your finances.
3. Your faith walk.

No matter what stage of pre-marriage or marriage you're in, these factors never go away. They're not just dealt with one time. They're continuously moving and make a big impact on your relationship together.

This first session is all about the past. We don't need to get into all the things you may have experienced or gone through in the past, but understand that they have formed who you are today and they may come up again and again in your married life.

Family, Friends, and Relationships

How was your family life before you got married? If you aren't married yet, realize that a lot of the things you do with your family may be really weird, awkward, or time-consuming. Do you and your spouse have different expectations when it comes to family gatherings? Do you play certain roles in your family that need to make some adjustments when you get married and start putting your spouse first? Does your significant other come from a large family in which they're used to having lots of people around all the time, or are you an only child and like having privacy?

It's funny sometimes to think of the families we come from. We really don't realize what kind of habits we've formed just from doing the same things with the same people our whole lives. Especially if there are cultural differences between you and your spouse, you may not realize the amount of adjusting you'll both need to do. It's not a bad thing, just something to take into consideration so you're each ready and able to adjust in the midst of new people and inside jokes you don't know about or understand.

Have you ever thought about the way you talk to your family, or the way they talk to you? It can be a real shock to head into someone else's home and be made fun of, because that's just how they interact and show love. Or maybe it's normal for them to be very loud and yell across rooms. Does one family hug and kiss as they enter each other's home while the other just says hi and smiles?

Every time Danrey and I sit with a new couple and talk about their family situations, we come away with so many laughs and stories to tell. They never realize that the way they've grown up has formed who they are and why they think and do the things they do. Again, these aren't bad things; they're just the normal day-to-day things people don't even think twice about.

Believe me, when you get married you'll notice all these things in your spouse. They do come out.

Danrey came from a very large Filipino family, and every event was celebrated largely. I came from a larger family, too, but we hardly ever got together and saw everyone. Only on certain occasions did we all try to come out, but it was okay not to get together very often.

My closest brother was seven years older than me and we didn't grow up in the same house, so I was by myself a lot. When Danrey and I were dating, he thought it would be fun to invite his brother and sister to come to our college and stay with us in our dorm rooms. Not only had I not had a sister at home with me, I'd also never had to share my room or my things.

So this was a challenge for me. When Danrey and I got married, the sleepovers with his siblings became more frequent, and sometimes they even invited their family friends to come over! The fun never stopped.

Literally two weeks into our marriage, I was exhausted and felt homesick. I missed my mom and the quiet house we'd had! I'm laughing as I write this… it sounds so silly, but it's very real.

We both realized that we depended on our parents' cooking as well, and we had a lot of recipes to learn in a short amount of time. We ate out a lot during our first month.

On a more serious note, we also had to learn how to speak our own language with each other. The way his parents spoke to him, the expectations they placed on him, and the cultural expectations, were all foreign to me. I talked to my mom like she was another girlfriend and we still are very close and often go out together. It would be completely weird if I didn't talk to her every day or plan to see her often. Danrey's siblings were still at home, his parents were still taking care of them, and their lives were very busy. So he didn't talk to them much.

Communication for me was important. But for him? Not so much. That was definitely something we had to work at. He wasn't used to talking about the day-to-day things, which proved detrimental later on in our marriage when he would keep to himself all the pressure and anxiety that was building up the inside. It led to arguments and sickness in his body.

The biggest thing we had to learn when we got married was making our own family plan and putting that first. It was like ripping off a band-aid. We had exposed all the painful and silly aspects of ourselves, and we chose to understand that these things had helped form who we were.

We then came to understand that some things couldn't stay the same. We needed to actively make our marriage better by speaking differently, by planning our days differently, and by being open to different options. I had now become one with this person and I could no longer look back to the way my family and I used to do things. We had to come up with a plan and do things our own new way—together!

What about friends? Our friends show us who we are. When you get married, you may have friends who aren't married yet—and that can be frustrating and genuinely painful. When it comes to these friends, there are three parties involved and all come to feel hurt. You don't get to have the same close-knit relationship with those friends anymore, and you spend less time together. Your spouse starts to feel guilty for taking you away from your close friends, and maybe you

Session One, The Past

start to feel a little resentful for not being able to do the things you used to do. Your priorities change.

It's okay to continue to have relationships with these friends, but you may have to establish boundaries with them. For examples, boundaries about how frequently they can come over to the house or limits on how often you go out with them and for how long.

When you get married, you choose your best friend—your spouse. You are always coming home to your spouse, and the decisions you make are going to affect your spouse.

I bring up other relationships here, too, because sometimes memories of past boyfriends or girlfriends will pop up. You may have experienced betrayal or hurt. A big part of you may have been lost in an old relationship, and this can play in your mind for years. You have to make a choice to shut that down and not take yourself down the wrong path with them. The internet has made it easy to see old faces and catch up with people you thought were gone from your life. It's never wise to dig up old romances or fill your head with images or pictures of them.

> SATAN CAN ATTACK YOU IN SO MANY SUBTLE WAYS. DON'T GIVE HIM AN INCH.

Satan can attack you in so many subtle ways. Don't give him an inch.

When we first got married, I had dreams about ex-boyfriends and I felt so guilty, because old feelings would come up. I prayed about this time and time again, and then in one dream I specifically remember saying to my ex, "Come. I would like you to meet my husband." I probably had that same dream a dozen times, but I haven't had it now for many years.

James 4:7 says, *"So humble yourselves before God. Resist the devil, and he will flee from you"* (NLT). I had to pray and ask God to help me with this, and then He gave me the words and the wisdom in a dream. How much more in everyday things does God want to be involved and help us out?

The most debilitating thing in marriage, I've found, is when you expect your spouse to act the same way as other people in your life. You have to get rid of the old thinking and old ways of doing things and learn new ways of communicating and showing love and affection to one another. The person you have married is worth making a clean slate for. Don't compare them to anyone you've previously been in a relationship with.

Take time to reflect and recognize how simple this first point is. Think about your family and relationships and how you can create your own new family routines and be willing to move from the past and into the present.

Finances

The way you've dealt with your own personal finances while you were single will definitely affect how you deal with finances in your marriage. A lot of people want to jump right into this topic, creating a vision for the future while forgetting that they've never worked on their finances with anyone else in mind but themselves. Every decision you've made with your finances in the past was only about you. No two people do everything the exact same way, and what you've been taught, or not taught, will affect how you think about finances in your marriage.

Some people like to ignore the topic altogether and assume that with two people they're simply doubling their income and will have more than enough every month to pay the bills.

But what happens when one spouse signs up to finance a purchase and doesn't think it's a big deal and then forgets to make payments on it? Or when your spouse reminds you, a few years into your marriage, that their student loan debt needs to be paid off now? Or when they go shopping and purchase items they think they need and nothing is left over for the rent the following day? Then what happens?

Some couples decide to keep their finances apart, even into their marriage. Their bank accounts, loans, investments, and credit cards stay separate. I've seen a lot of frustration when couples approach their finances this way.

The way Danrey and I looked at it, when we got married everything of mine became his and everything of his became mine. The Bible talks about two people becoming one. When I married him, I willingly took on all his student loans and he willingly took on my savings account… yep, true love!

The key to doing it that way, though, is to come to an understanding and make the choice to handle it together. We needed to work on our finances as a couple and both be aware of everything coming in and out of the account.

This area of our lives needed some work immediately. A lot of couples, like us, enter the engagement stage and spend so much time planning the wedding, spending lots of money and time on that, without putting the same amount of effort into financially planning for the rest of their lives. Then they wonder why they can't catch up or question where their money has gone.

If you aren't married yet, or even if you are, you can start from scratch today. Make the time to sit down together and decide not to form judgements about one another. Just listen to each other and talk finances. Think and talk about the ways you've handled money, or even thought of money in the past. Think and talk about the ways your parents have handled money and get a good picture of why they chose to operate that way.

For example, a friend of mine was always taught to pay her entire annual car insurance in a single payment when she received her tax return, and that way she didn't have to pay it monthly. I've followed her example, and I think it's the smartest way to do it. Danrey, on the other hand, liked the smaller monthly payments. But he also liked the buy-now-and-pay-later concept, or the don't-pay-for-a-year sales… they may give you what you want immediately, but they can sure give you a headache down the road.

Like I said, we had lots to work on and I'm sure you do, too. The first step was to recognize why we thought and acted the way we did with money, and recognize our good and bad habits.

Faith

How is your relationship with God? Are there certain routines you have or things you do when you're by yourself getting to know God more? What do you do when you want to pray? What church do you attend? How do you freely share your faith with others?

Being in a relationship with God is personal and will always be personal until you let another person in on your quiet time.

I woke up one morning a few days after we got married to the sound of video games being played. I love my quiet morning time with God, so I can start my day off on the right foot. My husband wasn't a morning person unless it was for video games or basketball. Now there was someone around infringing on my quiet time—and that was hard for me. I had to find myself a new routine.

Before we were married, Danrey was taking courses to become a youth pastor. He already had a position lined up at his church and was involved in some of the youth programs and worship team there. His church was smaller at the time and had an almost entirely Filipino congregation. Their services were held in a mixture of English and Tagalog.

At the time, I was attending a very large multicultural church and was involved in its financial administrative department. I enjoyed my church very much, but when I asked Danrey enough times to take me to his church, he finally took me and I literally fell in love with it. God really had a plan for me to go there and feel so welcome and find my place amongst a group of people in which I was always the outsider. I didn't speak their language, but when they spoke of the love of Jesus I knew what that was. When Danrey brought me to their youth group meetings, I immediately found my place and the rest was history.

My faith walk had to adjust to my new surroundings. I'm grateful that God gave me the peace I needed right away to make the move to a new church, environment, and culture.

At this stage in thinking about your own faith walk, it's really important to recognize that you actually have one. You've formed routines, habits, and especially theories that have created the foundation of your spiritual journey. You may have many questions about God and the Bible, and it's important to think about those things that are really important to you. Recognize that what's inside you is going to come out at some point. It will bring about conversations or heated debates in your marriage.

Danrey grew up in the church and was heavily involved in it, so that made our home prayer time non-existent. As I mentioned previously, I liked my own quiet time in the morning and sometimes would journal in the evenings before bed. That was kind of a foreign practice to him. We regularly prayed at our meals together, but that was it. He filled his hours praying for everything and everyone at church, to the point that I think he came home and thought he could just relax, whereas part of my relaxation came from praying.

We need to understand that everyone's faith level isn't at the same place. We don't have all the answers. God is personal and lives inside you. If you ask Him to lead and guide you and speak to you, He will. Your path won't be the same as everyone else's… and that's okay.

Being unequally yoked, as the Bible says, is a very real problem. I'm not suggesting you should find someone of the exact same level of faith, but you should be ready to grow together. If you're getting into a relationship and hoping that person will change, they won't. You might change instead. Are you okay with that?

There are a lot of people who come to Danrey and me well after their weddings, frustrated that their spouse isn't coming to church with them or that they don't even believe in God anymore. That's really hard to hear since they'd both come to pre-marriage counselling committed to each other and committed to God.

You need to talk to each other about your faith, what you believe, and the things you like to do. I enjoyed going to worship services, even at other churches and events. But Danrey, with his technical and drumming mind, could never get loose enough to worship with me and enjoy himself. I could go places and get so filled up only to have Danrey talk about how good the drummer had been, or how he wished we had those same lights and speakers they had. We had two totally different mindsets.

Thank God that today we understand each other and have learned to give and take in our own church. God may have called us, but He prepared us with years of training, of having heated discussions about why Danrey was so non-expressive in worship and prayer. I prayed about it, he has changed, and I have been happier in the process!

chapter eight

Session Two, The Present

THIS IS THE WORKING STAGE—THE PRESENT, THE TIME TO ACT. You have to understand that the present is always in effect. It's now, and when you get a few days, months, and years down the road, you will still be in the present.

You're at a point where the past is behind you and the future is ahead of you, but the decisions you make today will help put the past to rest and build a foundation for your future.

The hardest part at this stage is actually doing the work. A lot of people think that if it isn't broken, don't fix it; therefore, because they don't have trials and frustrations in these areas, they'll wait until they do before they do something about it.

That's the wrong approach. It's absolutely true that you cannot be prepared for everything that may come your way, but you can sure have some great tools in your belt when they do.

If you aren't actively working at certain areas of life, putting energy into them, they'll deteriorate. If we ignore our weight and just eat whatever we want whenever we want, we'll get to a place of frustration and break down our own self-esteem. It's a downward spiral.

The biggest thing we can share is to never stop talking. Having open communication about these areas is so important, especially for when they may be challenged later on. Build your foundation now, together.

Action for Your Relationships

Talk about your current family situation. Identify the relationships in your life that may have come up in the last chapter, ones you may need to talk about and plan for. Are there certain routines you have now, like taking care of parents or siblings, that could interfere with your own schedule as a married couple? Talk about how you can change these routines now so that the pressures don't get in the way of your marriage later on.

If you're already married, have you noticed areas in which you're putting other family members before your own spouse? If so, now is the time to address it. This will have definitely already become an issue in your marriage at some point. When you don't put your spouse first, it's really hard for your spouse to ever feel like they come first—and that's what God designed marriage to be, two people who become one—not one and a half.

Certain traditions or cultures may try to say otherwise. The Filipino culture is very family-oriented. Everything they do involves the whole family, and they assume you'll be a part of everything they want to do. Again, my family wasn't like that, so Danrey and I had to come to some sort of balance in the decisions we made concerning family trips, outings, and expectations. And since we were pastors in the church, we already had so much on our plate. This just seemed to frustrate everyone around us. We had to say no to so many gatherings, not because we didn't want to go but because we really had no time for ourselves at the end of the day.

In all your relationships right now, start to think of a plan, of a way for things to work better for you both. You'll come back to this over and over again. You'll constantly have to make decisions to be with your partner and put them before every other relationship.

Are there relationships in your life that may hinder your marriage? Take a step back and see who's around you right now. Who has influence in your life? Who speaks to you often and shares their own heart and life with you? People who are the closest to you should be those who won't get jealous or take sides or speak poorly of your partner. If they're constantly complaining or gossiping, you can guarantee they're doing the same about you; they will be toxic in your life and marriage.

Take a look at some of your own decisions when it comes to family, friends, or opposite-sex friendships. They probably don't feel the same anymore. Or you may notice that your partner has some relationships you may not fully agree with. You must talk about it and make a plan without judgement.

Recognize problems and do something about relationships and people who may be draining to your marriage. It's okay to distance yourself from people. I know we're always afraid of losing our friends, and we don't want that to happen, but we have decided to be with our spouses for the rest of our lives. That's a big decision and will require big steps and commitments. It always turns out to be the right decision. People will understand; everyone changes when they get married.

> YOU MUST TALK ABOUT IT AND MAKE A PLAN WITHOUT JUDGEMENT.

You must make the changes you can now. You'll have a better marriage relationship because of it.

Every marriage has arguments and disagreements. Right now you're at the stage where you talk about the problems that may have already surfaced and make a plan for how to have good fights. Danrey and I came up with our own words to speak to each other once an argument escalates to the point of no return. We say, "Too far." Upon hearing this, the other is supposed to know to stop. Then we are to keep quiet until we find a solution. No, it hasn't worked out perfectly every time, but adding this phrase to our vocabulary has prevented many arguments from escalating.

Make a game plan for when you have disagreements and come to an understanding to work through them. I found it unbelievably funny how many times we've had a disagreement while driving and our wedding song has come on the radio. God just knows. We've often broken out in laughter during arguments because of this.

You can weather any storm, if you both choose to.

Action for Your Finances

Now is the time to figure things out, to get rid of bad habits and make new and productive ones. It may be the simple act of sitting down together and hashing it out. You really can't look ahead to your future if you can't figure out what's going on in the present and make a plan.

If you're in the wedding planning stages, then those plans probably are on the forefront of your minds—where are you going to have the wedding, did you find the dress you want, where will the reception be, how many guests do you plan on inviting, how are you going to make invitations, where will you order the flowers from, how do you plan to pay for everything, etc. These are only a few of the costs of a wedding. It's really up to you how big you want your wedding to be. You don't have to do things the way everyone else seems to, especially if it means getting into debt over it. The truth of the matter is that the bride and groom are the ones to flip most of the bill in the end. It can be a real shock and stress producer.

The two of you are one, so the decision-making should come from both of you. Arriving at a real financial breakdown should be a priority. What are you willing to compromise in order to have a big wedding day? It's really only going to be one day of your lives, and when it's over you'll hold on to the memories. What do you want to remember—how you started off your marriage thousands of dollars in debt, or how that day really was a blessing for you in every way?

Danrey and I looked at our priorities in terms of what we wanted to have on our special day. For myself, all the basics were covered—the dress, the flowers, the wedding car, the cake, the giveaways, and I even made my own invitations. My husband rented his tux and we were going to have to pay for the hotel balance after the wedding. Our friends handled the videos and pictures. Because we decided on a lunch reception, the cost was nearly half of what it would have been if we'd chosen a dinner reception.

We thought we had all the bases covered, but there are thousands of dollars in little extras we didn't think about. Guaranteed, many of them you haven't thought about either. Hair, nails, new shoes, new purse, bachelor or bachelorette parties, extra food or drinks, coat room usage, family and bridal party gifts, centrepieces, decorations, thank-you cards, whatever is needed to book your honeymoon, etc. And never mind the reality that you'll be moving in together and trying to get your new place ready and liveable as well!

This is an important time for the two of you to start from scratch. Take the time to write out your monthly expenses, your quarterly and/or yearly expenses, and make note of the bills that will be coming up in the near and far future. Communicate about all expenses you may have acquired and all the new expenses you'll have together. Then write down your income and make a budget, both for the wedding and every day to follow. This could include loan payments that won't start until you're done school. And plan who's going to pay the bills. Whoever it is, both of you should be in the know when it comes to the account balances. When we're organized, we can have a lot of mental and physical peace.

Talk about the finances as much as you need to. If you're afraid to talk about buying groceries but aren't afraid to talk about getting into debt to purchase a home, you may be mixed-up… like we were.

It's so important to make plans and then pray and trust God with them. Thank Him for where you are right now, know that He wants the best for you, and trust that His blessing is for you. If you don't know what to do about your finances, Danrey and I encourage you to get help and ask questions. This doesn't have to be a time of embarrassment. Pray and ask God to show you the right person or couple to help you walk this out together. You will benefit from the help now and won't be frustrated later.

Make an action plan for yourselves now. Decide how much you're going to put into your wedding fund, and decide how much to put into a savings account.

Every idea is a good idea and an opportunity to hear each other out. You might not agree with every idea, and you're going to have to come up with solutions and compromises to show each other that you are *for* each other. You're a team and you'll work it out.

But I caution you not to move ahead with big financial decisions if you aren't both in agreement about them. Making decisions together can open the doors of your hearts to trust and be confident in one another. This is something you'll have to work out in your marital decision-making. Start from scratch, forget the former things, and look aheadYou may have to forgive each other and choose to forget past offences for the sake of building up your confidence and trust in one another again.

I remember going on dates and feeling like I was spoiled and swept off my feet. Danrey paid for everything and took care of me. But being married doesn't often feel like that. In fact, you may not go out on dates too often when you have to live on a budget. I often questioned where he got the money to pay for the expensive gifts he gave me, which definitely ruins the moment.

But you know what else ruins the moment? Getting the credit card bill in the mail afterwards. When that happened, Danrey would remind me how much I had loved the gift, but the look on my face was of death; I would slump around with a headache and fight not to say the words I really wanted to say.

I love my husband, but our decisions should bless each other with no financial burdens attached.

Making financial decisions will get easier when you work at it regularly. Danrey has gotten much better, and so have I. For a while he was the one in school and I was working. I provided everything we needed and I didn't realize what that did to his confidence. But we didn't talk about these important things. I didn't reassure and encourage him that he was a wonderful husband and that he was doing as much for our marriage as I was.

Make your plan today!

Action for Your Faith

Keep your faith in motion. Don't stop praying together. Don't stop going to church together. Get on the same page when it comes to giving. And don't stop believing.

Again, it's time to talk about your faith. Now that you're together and moving forward in your relationship, think about your church life, personal worship, and devotion times and how you're going to make a plan for your marriage. You bring God's strength into your marriage—if you want to. You can rely on God's love to fill you so you can fill each other—if you want to.

It's so important for you to know that how much you want to open yourself up to God is completely up to you. As Revelation 3:20 says, *"Here I am! I stand at the door and knock. If anyone hears my voice and opens the door, I will come in and eat with that person, and they with me."*

God is the one who created marriage, and now the world is trying to confuse it with so many different options and choices. But the truth is that if God created it—and you can see that in the Bible—then there must be great significance and importance to it. You actually enter into a blood covenant with each other and God. He made it that way. There are blessings attached to the covenants God has made and you need to know about them. The marriage bed is blessed. God wants you to do things His way because there are great blessings for you when you do!

Because God has created marriage, should you not put Him at the forefront of it? The truth is that when the storms of life come, when people become too busy, they forget that God has a perfect plan for them, one that won't let them live in frustration or fear but in peace and joy all the days of their lives. You may say this is impossible, but I know the calming peace in the midst of the storm. Don't be quick to panic or worry. Stay calm and just know deep down that everything is going to be okay.

You need to make time to pray together every day. Go to church regularly and get involved together. You need a strong community of encouragement around you.

This same advice could be included in the financial section, too. When you make a plan and give your tithe and offering, know that those are seeds for your future! God calls the tithe obedience to Him. It's a way of showing that you trust His blessing is on the rest of your money. When you do this as a couple, you take the pressure off each other to be the financial provider of your home. You should both trust that God is protecting and leading you into great blessings and will take care of your every need as you put your hands to work.

You aren't always going to feel like going to church or getting involved in a praise or worship night, but help each other make a plan together. Encourage each other in what you like to do and always encourage each other in ways to grow your faith. Make plans to attend marriage conferences, and purchase material that will help you in your marriage.

Remember, this is the working stage. You have all the moving parts in front of you and you get to make every effort now to build a solid foundation in your marriage.

Growing and learning in your faith life will always benefit your marriage. As you both learn and become closer to God, who created you and knows you from the inside out, you will also grow closer to one another. You will learn how to understand each other better. You'll be more patient and kind to one another. You'll have peace and not only enjoy your marriage but enjoy your lives.

> YOU HAVE ALL THE MOVING PARTS IN FRONT OF YOU AND YOU GET TO MAKE EVERY EFFORT NOW TO BUILD A SOLID FOUNDATION IN YOUR MARRIAGE.

If you're a couple people want to be around, that means you're doing something right! Don't just sit and let another day go by without taking steps to grow your faith. If you keep moving, your relationship will grow as well.

The more intimate Danrey and I are with Jesus, the more intimate we are with each other. After seventeen years of marriage, we are connected on such a deep level. It has evolved our love and how we show it to each other. God created that in us. Our desire for each other just grows stronger as we put more time and effort into our marriage.

chapter nine

Session Three, The Future

TALKING TO COUPLES ABOUT THE *PAST* CAN BE INTERESTING AND tricky. Talking to couples about the *present* can be tedious and daunting. But talking to couples about the *future* is absolutely exciting!

Every couple has big hopes for the future and has put much thought and daydreaming into it. Whether it be the wedding day plans or upcoming vacations, or new jobs or homes or children, everyone is excited to talk about the future.

You cannot have a vision for your future without taking the steps to secure your foundation. Otherwise your future remains a daydream, and you become like a hamster on a wheel that goes nowhere.

Your Relationship Future

You can have great relationships with your family, in-laws, and friends. After putting those needed boundaries in place, you actually enjoy those relationships more and feel like you have the freedom to choose. You don't have to dread future events, outings, get-togethers, vacations, or even unexpected living situations.

Agree to be open about having each other's back. People will come and go in your life and you have to be able to talk about what they bring to your relationship. New co-workers will come along, you'll have new challenges, and you need to be on guard and determine to be open and talk about these things.

It's extremely unfortunate to hear of couples divorcing after years of marriage. We hear that they lose interest in each other, or life gets into a routine and there's no excitement anymore. This happens to people who have disengaged from each other for a long time. Divorce is never the result of a single thought that comes up one day and is acted upon; it's something that's been seeded and allowed to grow.

Some couples take steps right from the start to get into counselling to make sure they're not in that position later. They work on their marriages right away. Not all of us have done that, but we can pray and work on our relationship daily. Little things will make the biggest impact.

You've already made the decision to limit time with some people and learned better ways to help each other when it comes to your family. Together you are a team and will continue to work together and make the adjustments needed, always putting each other first.

We didn't know that our future would include living with both sets of in-laws. We had to take what we'd learned and put it into action daily. We made these times of living with family enjoyable and determined to make our family unit stronger in the process.

And then there's a whole other aspect to your future: children!

Many couples dream and plan for their children, even naming them, before they come along. But I want to warn you: you need a family plan when thinking about your future and children. This is an area where your old habits may come out, habits related to how you grew up and what your parents instilled in you. Many people will speak into your life and family, and you have to know how to filter it. If you're thinking about having children—plan for *your* future, not necessarily theirs.

Once our first son was born and he was wheeled into my hospital room, I froze and my stomach flipped. We had to grow up that day. Literally, we weren't prepared to be parents and all that it would entail.

Having had four children now, I think we've figured a few things out. But we still have to plan day by day, filtering what everyone else tells us and planning for our future. With the foundation we've created as a husband and wife, including the continual work we do on ourselves and our relationships, we can dream and plan for our future together.

Your Financial Future

Now that you have so much written out and nothing is hidden anymore, you can dream and make plans for the future.

You'll have a sense of accomplishment once you've made a budget and a plan. This will enable you to see and make goals. Having goals for your business or employment will give you stability and vision. Goals for repaying debt will give you a vision of how life will look when those loans are paid off. Maybe you need to do some house planning, or vacation planning or travel planning.

We want you to be free from anxiety when it comes to finances and not base your vision on your limited income and thinking. God promises to take care of you, to lead and guide you, and He has a great commission for you. You have been created with special gifts and talents. You have dreams in your heart that have come from Him. You need to know that it's okay to listen to God, the Holy Spirit in you, and follow the desires of your heart.

What is not okay is failing to see the future with your spouse in mind. God created you both and the vision you strive for needs to have both spouses involved in it.

Your financial future can be great because of the steps you take in the present. Every day you have the choice to stick to the budget, to pay off debt, to save money, and to give money away and sow seeds. But everything you choose will set you up for your future. Be mindful, be determined, and be a visionary for your family.

One thing I love doing is writing down my goals and making a vision board. I've gotten over the fact that some people think it's silly and a waste of time. I'm okay with that.

I have taught my family about vision and the importance of writing down our dreams and desires. The first year I started doing it with my family, we accomplished seven of the ten things that were on the list. Not only did we write things down and pray about them together often, we check-marked all the things we had accomplished.

It was so beneficial for my children to see that some of the things seemed impossible… and yet they happened. And some of the things happened in such an unusual way that even my kids knew that God must have had His hand in it.

The three things we didn't accomplish weren't forgotten about, and we continue to thank God for them. We also know that some of them can't happen at this time. We don't own the home we live in at the moment, so we can't get the kitty and puppy the kids would like.

As a couple, you determine your future. God has a plan for you and it's good, according to Jeremiah 29:11.

As you connect with God and each other, you will see that with God nothing is impossible for you. There are no finances in heaven, so never think that God doesn't care about you just because He doesn't rain money down from the sky. You need to take the first step and trust God with your wealth. If you do, opportunities will open up that you never thought possible. God is setting you up and will use people to give you favour in the least favourable situations. That's how good He is!

> *Now to him who is able to do immeasurably more than all we ask or imagine, according to his power that is at work within us, to him be glory in the church and in Christ Jesus throughout all generations, for ever and ever! Amen.*
> —Ephesians 3:20–21

Your Faith Future

I knew my husband was going to school to be a youth pastor, but we never gave any thought to that would look like, nor did we imagine pastoring our own church one day. We didn't take the time to dream and envision our future.

When I got involved in the youth program, I really found my place—and once that transferred into the women's ministry, everything began to snowball. We started running most of the programs offered at our church, plus I had a job, and at this time we were starting to have children. We let a lot of other people dictate who we were and who we were to become.

But there came a day when we laid it all down and told God we couldn't do it anymore. All these activities were robbing us of our joy and peace, because we hadn't dreamed and envisioned it as part of our own future. If you don't dictate your own future, something or someone will.

When our marriage began to fall apart, we took a step back and asked God to take over. And then when that pastor's word was spoken over us and we had more children, it was like a breath of fresh air. God was still at work in our lives. It was time to get back to our roots, seek Him, and plan our own future together. We gained a vision for our lives, and all the stress and anxiety started to fall off. It was like every heavy weight and chain fell off. We weren't only lighter; we were alive!

If God created you and created marriage, don't you think He has a great future for you?

I encourage you to dream about your future. Talk about the desires that are in your heart. Though they may be silly or weird to talk to each other about, the process will be beneficial for you both. You have to let out your big and small dreams without being afraid of putdowns or discouragement.

I have to trust that my husband hears me and is being led by God just like I am, and hearing him out and encouraging him will both bless him and bless our marriage as well. I am better when he is better. We can encourage each other. When we disconnect with God, we make bad choices and let our guard down. When we disconnect in our marriages, we make bad choices and let our guard down.

Session Three, The Future

Your faith future includes learning how to turn each other towards Jesus and encouraging one another to focus on Jesus and grow in Him daily.

The number one secret I've learned, which continues to show itself strong, is prayer. Women have a powerful spiritual connection that will change a man's heart and mind! Yes, it works the other way, too, but I have noticed that if Danrey and I aren't on the same page about something, or if I have a great idea but am not sure he will like it, I will pray about it and give it over to God. No joke, within a week at most Danrey will come to me and talk about the exact same thing or tell me he had been thinking about such and such… and it will be exactly what I prayed about.

I've also noticed that when I pray about something, I go into prayer not with the mindset of having it done *my* way. Instead I pray about the circumstance or situation working out in the best way possible. Danrey then often comes to talk to me about that issue and together we come up with an even greater plan or vision than what I had in mine.

You need each other! You will have the best outlook for your lives when you talk together and take it to God as a couple.

> *Again I say unto you, That if two of you shall agree on earth as touching any thing that they shall ask, it shall be done for them of my Father which is in heaven.*
> —Matthew 18:19, KJV

You are a powerful team!

It's so important that you look beyond everything in the natural and grow in Christ daily, for His supernatural and miraculous works are for you today. Dream big together. Catch a vision for your marriage and your life.

Take delight in the Lord, and he will give you the desires of your heart.

—Psalm 37:4

Where there is no vision, the people perish...
—Proverbs 29:18, KJV

chapter ten

Never Give Up

I BELIEVE YOU AS A COUPLE ARE READING THIS TODAY, WHETHER you're just starting out or are just starting again, because you have hope for your future together. God created you and gave you the choice to be in the marriage you're in. Danrey and I are not counsellors, but we have a heart to share our story and the message God has given us to help encourage you.

Letting go of the past, actively coming to terms with where you are right now, and building your foundation on the rock (Christ Jesus) will give you everything you need to succeed in your marriage and in your life!

God knows everything about your past—and whether it be together or separate, He loves you just the same and will be your guide. We don't believe that spouses fall in and out of love, but that it's a choice they make. Stick with the choice to love.

I heard some great advice one day for couples who have struggled with a partner in areas of addiction. The person said to look at your partner as a brother or sister in Christ. If we would see them that way, our hearts would change towards them. We would want to help, hear, and not take everything so personally. We would also celebrate with them more through all their victories, big and small.

After much frustration and deceit in our marriage, I have learned to thank God and pray for my husband more. I have also spoken scriptures over myself which declare what God says about me. I don't rehearse the thought of not trusting my husband. In fact, I say, "God, I trust You with him."

Praying has brought a lot of peace and great change to our marriage relationship. Instead of my speaking exactly what I think in the heat of the moment, I have learned to take a deep breath, take it all to God, and let Him fill me with peace. I have also found many ways to encourage and build up my husband as the man God has made him as the head of our home.

> YOUR MARRIAGE AND ITS SUCCESS IS YOUR DECISION.

Your marriage and its success is your decision. You can conquer any storm and have an amazing life together! Never give up on God and each other; He will make a way where there seems to be no way.

If it is possible, as far as it depends on you, live at peace with everyone [especially your spouse].

—Romans 12:18

A new command I give you: Love one another. As I have loved you, so you must love one another [especially your spouse].

—John 13:34

See, I am doing a new thing [in your marriage]! Now it springs up; do you not perceive it? I am making a way in the wilderness and streams in the wasteland.
—Isaiah 43:19

Be kind and compassionate to one another [in your marriage], forgiving each other [often], just as in Christ God forgave you.
—Ephesians 4:32

Bear with each other and forgive one another if any of you has a grievance against someone. Forgive as the Lord forgave you [in your marriage].
—Colossians 3:13

I encourage you to personalize God's Word. It was spoken for you and applies to your life today. His Word has power and is power. When you speak it out over your marriage, family, and circumstances and believe what it says, those areas of your life will be affected.

When God created the world He spoke things into being:

And God said, "Let there by light," and there was light.
—Genesis 1:3

The spoken Word is Christ Himself:

In the beginning was the Word, and the Word was with God, and the Word as God.
—John 1:1

When you invite Christ into your life, He will dwell inside you. As you speak His Word (who He is) and believe (are fully convinced that what He said is the final authority), you will have those things that you say.

> *Therefore I tell you, whatever you ask for in prayer, believe that you have received it, and it will be yours.*
>
> —Mark 11:24

The more you read the Bible, the Word of God, the more you will believe what it says in terms of renewing your mind to think like Christ first. You need the Word of God in your life daily. You are working on your marriage when you get into the Word of God.

> *For the word of God is alive and active. Sharper than any double-edged sword, it penetrates even to dividing soul and spirit, joints and marrow; it judges the thoughts and attitudes of the heart.*
>
> —Hebrews 4:12

> *…so is my word that goes out from my mouth: it will not return to me empty, but will accomplish what I desire and achieve the purpose for which I sent it.*
>
> —Isaiah 55:11

> *For no matter how many promises God has made, they are "Yes" in Christ. And so through him the "Amen" is spoken by us to the glory of God.*
>
> —2 Corinthians 1:20

Believe in God and in each other, position yourself to hear from God, and invite Him to work in your marriage daily.

I can do all this through him who gives me strength.
—Philippians 4:13

Our marriage is our own perfect team!

Also by the Author

The Promised Child
978-1-4866-1649-7

Danrey and Christie Amoyo knew that they wanted to be parents, but when their happy announcement turned into the worst possible scenario they found out that becoming parents was not to be an easy path for them.

This book is a written testimony of how determination, coming from a new revelation of faith, can change lives. It will demonstrate that the promises we read about in the Bible are for us today, even if we don't yet know how they apply to the situations we're living through.

Be encouraged by the Amoyos' experience as, after years of heartbreak and loss, the Word becomes real and they put their faith first.

Crayons, Crumbs, and Christian Growth
ISBN: 978-1-4866-1714-2

Parenting children is a wonderful blessing that comes with great challenges. As you navigate the waters of parenthood, it can be easy to feel disconnected from life and your faith. You may think you are alone on this journey, and you may be frustrated trying to meet the demands all around you.

But these years can be the greatest of your life—years in which God shows you how real He is, how faith actually works, and how you can enjoy the blessings He's given you. In *Crayons, Crumbs, and Christian Growth*, Christie shares about how the trials and treasures of parenting her own children has taught her so much about who God is.